Don't Get Fat, Kids!

100 quips about life from a middle-aged husband and father

Michael J. Stanuszek

To my beautiful and loving wife, Mandy,
and our two wonderful kids,
Gracie and Huckleberry.

Coaching boys soccer this morning. Halfway through the first quarter, the referee looks at me, points to my players, and says, "Getting a little handsy, aren't they?"

I respond, "You know, my wife said the same thing to me on our first date. And we both know how that night ended, don't we? [wink]"

The referee left me alone the rest of the game.

House is quiet. Lights are out. Kids and wife are sound asleep. I'm lying here in bed at 10:53 on a Wednesday night wondering if it's too late to order a pizza.

When I die and meet my creator, I'm going to have a hell of a lot to answer for. But, I'm confident that while I'm standing there at those pearly gates, and St. Peter is reading off the list of my transgressions, the Good Lord will pull me to the side and whisper in my ear, "Those calendars that your daughter's Catholic school is pushing you to sell to family and friends for $36.50 apiece, I would've refused to sell them, too. On that one, you get a pass."

Much like my first sexual experience, that eclipse was a lot of build up for about two and a half minutes of disappointment.

That time when you showed up to the school's meet & greet 30 minutes early, but the buffet line was already open so you helped yourself to three helpings before the next adult had their first, and then your wife shows up an hour later only to greet you with, "Hey, I heard some asshole got here early just to eat all the food! You know who it was?" "No, I saw him though," I said. "Really obnoxious eater!"

Imagine my surprise when I found my old high school varsity jacket on sale at the local thrift store (apparently, my wife had donated it week prior). It was priced at $3. $3!?! I said to the lady working there, "Lady, you know what this is? This is an authentic Owosso High School varsity jacket. From 1997, no less! Two varsity letters. That's right, two! Sure, one was for marching band, but it still counts! This jacket is worth more than $3." She says, "Sir, this jacket has your name on it. Not a lot of people with the name 'Stanuszek' walking around East Tennessee." I responded, "Lady, there are starving children in [note at this point, I'm wondering to myself where I'm going with this conversation] South Africa that would die for this jacket." She responded, "Really?!? South Africa? Year-round temperature of 108 and they want a heavy jacket?" I said, "These colors don't run, lady! Don't run!!!" She responded, "I don't know what that even means."

At this point, I realize that I was going head to head with the smartest thrift store worker ever, and we weren't getting anywhere. I dropped my $3 on the counter and walked out, jacket in hand. So if you see me driving around this afternoon wearing my varsity jacket proudly, don't think me a fool.

Wife tells me I'm looking for recommendations for a penis doctor for a vasectomy. Wife tells me I need to have the surgery done within the next 30 days. Wife tells me if there aren't any penis doctors available that soon, then I'll take anyone with a doctorate degree: chiropractor, eye doctor, dentist, English lit professor, etc. Wife tells me that this is ultimately my decision, but she's going to withhold certain marital privileges until the surgery is done. Wife is persuasive when she wants to be.

Fellas, when your woman asks you to watch the movie the "Notebook" with her in exchange for her giving you some "quality time" later in the evening, don't be fooled. In the last scene of the movie, the husband and wife die in bed while cuddling. Trust me, ain't nothing going on after the end of that movie other than your woman wanting to have a little "quality time" cuddling.

When the gym runs out of towels just before you've exited the whirlpool, don't try to dry your whole body off with a blow dryer. There are parts of a man's body that do not react well to intense, concentrated heat.

So last weekend, I posted a picture on Facebook of my half naked body draped over my mom's piano (in my most seductive pose) in an effort to sell it. Lawyers, judges, and other court personnel who saw my post gave me shit about it all week. Well, a guy from back home (who would not have otherwise known about the piano) saw my post, contacted me for my mom's number, and went and looked at the piano today. Piano sold, bitches!

On a related note, if anyone out there is having a hard time selling their household goods and is looking for a new marketing approach, I take Visa.

My daughter gets $5 a week to do the dishes each night. Tonight, I secretly watched her demonstrate for her little brother how she does them. I thought, "God, she's teaching him something new. She's so sweet; far too sweet to be mine. She's just like her mother. Does she have any of my personality at all?" Five minutes later, I overheard her tell her little brother that she'll give him $1 a week to do the dishes each night. I thought, "There I am."

My wife is into this new Netflix show, GLOW. GLOW, of course, stands for "Gorgeous Ladies of Wrestling;" the show is a look at women's pro wrestling from the 1980's. I think it's pretty cool that she's showing an interest in pro wrestling (a favorite of mine), but I have to admit, spending an hour in the pool trying to stop my wife from putting me in the camel clutch makes for a long afternoon.

Marriage: a relationship where the husband is expected to apologize to his wife for something that he did in her dream the night before.

I can't quite convince myself to trust my kid with a bottle of ketchup around household furniture, but I don't think twice on the Fourth of July about handing her a sparkler burning at 2,000 degrees.

Before going to bed, Huck leans over and whispers to me, "Daddy, I can't wait to see Sophia at Disney World tomorrow." "Oh son," I replied. "Sophia is a show on Nickelodeon. I don't think she'll be at Disney." "No daddy," he says. "Sophia from Mommy's show, the Golden Girls."

Woke up in the middle of the night to some shuffling at the end of my bed. Still half asleep, I saw the silhouette of a long, skinny object dancing up and down and back and forth. It was taunting me; intimidating me. I lie motionless for three minutes trying to control my fear. Perhaps if I was fully awake, I would've figured out it was just my cat's tail; however, my brain immediately went with cobra. Spent the next ten minutes upset with my cat that he let a cobra into our house. Then woke the wife up to let the cobra out. Spent the rest of the night sleeping on the couch.

As I was lounging (alone) in the gym pool tonight, I couldn't help but notice that the attractive woman in the skimpy outfit running on the treadmill overlooking my position was undressing me with her eyes. I'm a married man, so obviously I couldn't let this stand. I gave her a look so as to say "Married man here. Nothing to see, lady." She persisted, licking her lips and batting her eyes. I then held up my left hand to show off my wedding band, but it only made her more brazen. She flipped her hair and giggled like a school girl. I was getting desperate to make her stop; I'm not a piece of meat. Finally, I thought, "I'll just go over there and tell her that perhaps if we had met at a different time, a different place, it may have been different. I'll let her off easy." So, I swam over to the pool ladder, paused for a second to soak up the moment, and then lifted my hulking, huge ass out of the pool. And wouldn't you know it?!? That did the trick all by itself. She quickly jumped off the treadmill and exited stage left.

My fat ass - saving me from awkward moments one woman at a time....

So, I'm undressing at the gym, and a group of 10-year-old boys walks into the locker room. I'm going to assume that their dad's "Boys, don't laugh!" comment was pure coincidence.

At my 3-year-old son's tee-ball game. The boy cried every time the ball was hit to someone else, he threw his bat at the home plate ump after he attempted the world's first tee-ball bunt, he tried to round the bases by initially going in the wrong direction (third base to first base), and perhaps most impressive, he committed 8 errors in a 25-minute game. Got the game ball.

Watching the NFL draft as a Lions fan is like waking up on Christmas morning as a little kid knowing that all your shiny, new presents are going to be broken in a year.

My kid is having a slumber party tonight. Six little kids. Little girl comes up to me and says, "Do you have a brother?" "Sure do," I replied. Complete lie. She says, "Ok, that makes sense. My dad always talks about 'Sexy Stu' and 'Fat Stu.' Your brother must be the sexy one, I guess."

After dinner, I rinsed my plate, which didn't rise to my daughter's standards, so she re-rinsed my plate, which didn't rise to my wife's standards, so she re-re-rinsed my plate. Fellas, if this happens, and your wife then asks you what can be learned from this experience, the answer is never, "Give your wife the plate to rinse first."

As we sat down for Easter service this morning, I gave my 3-year-old son a stern look followed by a two-finger point to my eyes and then a two-finger point to his. You know the look - the one that lets him know that I'm watching his every move. It felt good; I had secured my place in the pecking order of the family. The dad. The disciplinarian. The head of the family. I had exercised my dominance over my son. And then about two hours later, my eight-year-old daughter caught me looking for Easter candy, and she gave me the same look and finger point.

We have a rule in our house that I'm not allowed to touch my kids' Easter basket candy for the two hours after they wake up. Then, it's a free for all. This morning, my kids made the fatal mistake of going for the giant chocolate bunny that's been conspicuously placed on top of the basket, leaving all the jelly beans, jolly ranchers, and peanut butter cups below completely untouched. One day they'll learn that the chocolate bunny is a sucker bet; no matter how badly they want it to be solid, the damn thing is always going to be hollow. But today, my kids are going to learn a lesson, and in another three minutes, I get to bathe in a sea of Cadbury Eggs.

Lots and lots of prom pics on my fb wall this morning. All the kids dressed up and looking so innocent and angelic; like they wouldn't do anything wrong. I don't know about you, but I remember taking similar pics before my prom(s), and the thoughts going through my head at the time were anything but innocent and angelic.

They say teams assume the personality of their coach. This morning, our opponents wore matching cleats, socks, shin guards, and bows in their hair; they did synchronized pre-game calisthenics, and their team name was "White Lightening." My team, on the other hand, had two girls who forgot their shin guards, one who forgot her socks, our pre-game calisthenics was some variation of Duck Duck Goose, and our team name (as picked by the girls) was "Carrot Juice Easter Bunnies." And while we may have loss 22-1, I told my girls after the game that if the scoreboard measured how much fun each team had, it would've easily - EASILY - been closer to 22-6.

Going to the "I love the 90's concert" tonight with the wife. She told me to dress like the 90's. Took her advice. I'm wearing my outfit from last Tuesday.

I went to the gym today but forgot my after-workout clothes at home. So, after my workout, I changed back into my suit, but had to walk out without wearing any underwear or an undershirt. My wife was home alone. The kids were at school. So, of course, I'm thinking, "I'll surprise the Mrs. at home with a little 'Magic Mike' dance number and see where the afternoon goes." Everything was going according to plan too until the wife realized what was happening. She laughed. She laughed hard. I pictured the afternoon going in a different direction.

Signs you may have spent too much time in a men's locker room:

My eight-year-old daughter: "Daddy, I really need to take a sh..."

Me: "Whooaaaaaa.... Don't you dare finish that word. We don't cuss, little lady!"

Daughter: "What word? Shower?!?"

My son loves to put his hands in his pockets. He recently learned that if he unzips his fly, that creates another pocket for his hands. Makes for some fantastic looks while at the grocery store.

If these sons of bitches think I'm gonna pay $50 for school pics, they're crazy. I do like the proofs, though. They were free. I'm thinking that with a little lamination, we got five 2x3 pics for the living room here. No one looks at wallets anyway.

It's hard to diet when you're married to a woman who can cook. Really hard! I tried to explain my predicament to my wife by equating it to how she must feel when I take my shirt off at the end of the night, and she has to control her unbridled urge to rub my chest and abs. Simply impossible.

She started laughing. She hasn't stopped. That was an hour ago.

Diet Day 10. Found myself loitering in the frozen food section of the grocery store. May have mouthed "I miss you" to a 64 pack of pepperoni pizza rolls. Walking out of the store, I felt like that gal lying on the door in the movie "Titanic." I'll never let you go.....

We're all allowed to forget a detail or two from New Year's Eve. You know, like when you forget that your wife, Mandy, thought it'd be funny to change the name associated with your law firm's phone number on caller ID.

So, if anybody got a call this week from "The Jerk Store," give me a shout tomorrow.

When mommy does the kids' Christmas shopping and wraps all the presents too, daddy is just as surprised to see what's under the tree as the kids.

"We spent how much?!?"

I just heard Prince's "Cream" for the first time in like 25 years. Having now listened to it, I don't think that song means what I thought it meant back when I was in junior high. I'm also questioning that Thanksgiving at grandma's house when I played that song during family dinner.

Caught a glimpse of my naked body in the full-length mirror at the gym today. Immediately felt compelled to text my wife an apology.

I don't think women realize just how easy it is to Christmas shop for men. I mean, I get asked for suggestions by women all the time, and it always amazes me that there's any confusion. So, I figure I'll just set the record straight here. Ladies, no matter what your guy is into, and no matter what he's asked for, the answer is always a black teddy.

Also, if someone could pass this post onto my wife, I'd appreciate it. I've been asking for the same thing for 14 years now, but I keep getting socks.

I said "Spike Tv," but my old man - who never watches television - thought I said "Spank Tv." I figure I can get 48 hours of fun out of this before I have to tell him the truth.

Hey skinny people, you had your season already - it's called summer. And while you might refer to the last two seasons of the year as fall and winter, today marks the beginning of an extended period-of-time that us full figured people call "good eatin" season. So, enjoy your 4th of July parties in your skimpy bathing suits with your toned abs. Today is Thanksgiving, bitches. It's our Super Bowl!

Anyone else got a three-year-old that punches him in the junk to determine if he's sleeping or not? The kid's method is fool proof, actually. He's never found daddy sleeping, ever.

I'm not saying that I've set the bar too low, but my sister did just say our parents would be impressed with any anniversary gift from me north of $10 Burger King gift cards.

Wife is out of town. She called this morning to ask what I fed the kids last night for dinner after we went trunk-or-treating. I asked wife if she understands that free candy is given away at trunk-or-treating.

Sure, I have fun watching my kids trick or treat. But I have way more fun watching my daughter school my son in candy cattle trading when we get home. Jesus Christ, she just bullied him into trading an Almond Joy and a Mounds for three Snickers Bars. Then, recognizing his inexperience, she told him that her pencil (nobody wants a damn pencil!) was a rocket ship, and she got some fruit snacks out of it. She is just owning him right now! This is gonna get out of hand quickly.

Wife: "Stu, Stu, Stu! Wake up!!!!! It's freezing in our living room! I think the furnace is out!!!"

I walk to the living room.

I close the window she left open the night before.

I walk back to bed.

I went by the Halloween store tonight to pick up some Halloween candy, and I couldn't help but notice its impressive collection of women's Halloween costumes. I had my eye on this skintight Wonder Woman outfit complete with a built-in padded bustier, hip hugging shorts, knee high vinyl boots, and a rope for tying up whatever the lady pleases. I thought, "You know what? My children really should see my wife for the super hero that she is every day." So, I reckon I might just mosey on down there tomorrow and buy that outfit for my wife. You know, for the children.

Just a gut feeling, but I feel like we'd have more leverage to argue in this upcoming parent/teacher conference if we had shown up on the right day. Could be wrong.....

My kid was going to play tag in gym class today. So, I told her a little white lie on the way to school that her daddy was the "grand master wizard of a group of tag players growing up. But she had to keep it a secret." Harmless enough, I thought. Until the end of the day when she admitted that she had told people all day that her daddy was the "grand wizard of this special group of people. But it's a secret."

Ummmmm.....

My son can't figure out the toilet yet but can name all the fast food joints from here to daddy's office. That's some next level parenting right there!

Wife asked me what I want for our anniversary. I told her "something with an underwire," thinking she would understand that I was suggesting that she buy herself some lingerie. Her response of "do they make men's boxer briefs with an underwire now?" makes me think that I'm not getting shit.

I asked my two-year-old son, who's sitting in the living room, to put his sippy cup in the kitchen sink. But instead of walking into the kitchen, he throws his sippy cup ten feet (in the general direction of the kitchen) and yelled, "Nailed it!"

Marriage.

Me: "You doing okay, babe?"

Wife (as she's walking by): "My back really hurts, and I've been bending over the last hour giving Huck his bath."

Me: "Well, why don't you get the boy out of his bath and put him to bed early. I'll meet you in our bedroom. I'll close the shades and light some candles, put a little Lionel Ritchie on the radio, and give you something special that'll last 'all night long.' [wink]. Something that'll make your back feel no pain, if you know what I mean?"

Wife (as she continues walking by): "Oh, thanks honey. Tylenol would be great."

Wife says yesterday, "Let's Go to O'Charley's for Mother's Day." Now, my only experience with this place was during law school some 15 years ago, when the entire school would take over the one on the strip three nights a week, and the only thing I ordered - the only thing any of us ever ordered - were $1.00 46 oz beers. To this day, I thought the place was a bar, not a restaurant. So, when the wife said yesterday that we were going to O'Charley's today, I thought "Hot damn! Day drinking on Mother's Day! Let's get a babysitter and make some bad decisions."

Eating quiche from a buffet bar is not the way I pictured this day going.

I don't think women realize how hard it is for us married men. Believe it or not, there are women out there who are attracted to men just because they're married. They see his wedding ring, and some switch goes off. It's like an aphrodisiac. Take me, for example. I'm as married as a man gets. Throw in my full head of hair, my world-class ass, and the straightest teeth this side of the Mississippi, and it's amazing that I manage to get through the day unsullied by one of these vixens. So be nice to your married men, ladies. They're dealing with a lot out there.

Noticed the boy was playing with his toy screwdrivers this morning. So, I set out to explain to him the difference between his flat head screw driver and his Phillips head screwdriver. We discussed the handle, the shaft, the tip, the blade, the recess, the angle. We quizzed. We tested. We quizzed again. After 20 minutes, he knew the difference between the two screwdrivers, and he was referring to them correctly. Proud Dad moment! Went back in there 30 minutes later. He's still playing with his toy screwdrivers. He's referring to one as the "daddy screwdriver" and one as the "mommy screwdriver."

My girls' soccer teams were short a player tonight, so I filled in at midfield for our scrimmage.

Me: "There's no way an old, fat man like me should score on you girls!!!!"

Player: "Coach, that's not fair!!! You're a middle-aged, fat man!!!"

So, I'm at this little league game, and all the parents seem to be so supportive of their boys - no matter whether they're doing well or not. "Good job, Johnny!" "Great effort, Bobby!" "Nice try, Timmy!" You know, maybe it was just me, but I distinctly remember my old man giving me the business from the sidelines every time I messed up in a little league game. Just heckling the shit out of me. Like every game. Like with signs. Not saying today's approach to kids is any better (or worse) than my dad's, but I can say for certain that it's a hell of a lot easier getting my teeth kicked in by a pissed off judge having had a dad who yelled "E6" at me from the third base line for 10 years.

Watching a dating show with the wife. If these shows really wanted to see how compatible two people are in a long-term relationship, they should sit them at a kitchen table with a budget and a stack of bills and have them talk it out over a couple of tuna fish sandwiches.

Daughter: "Daddy, what does Justin Timber-Blake mean when he says, 'I'm bringing sexy back'? What is sexy?"

Me: "Oh, ummmm. 'Sexy' is the name of his dog. The dog got out of his backyard. He's bringing him back home."

Daughter: "Ohhhh. Ok, what does it mean when Justin Timber-Blake says, "You see these shackles. Baby, I'm your slave"?

Me: "It means Justin Timber-Blake is a sick son of a bitch, and you're listening to country music from now on!"

Standing in the back of church because we arrived late this morning. Choir in the front is singing a soft, slow, somber song. People are praying. Priest is pacing about. All is quiet, except my children who are basically treating the back of church as their personal romper room. My wife, Mandy, having spent 50 straight minutes corralling these two, has what I would call "a mental break." She bows her head, clears her throat, and then - in her outdoor voice - looks at me and exclaims, "Day-o. Daaaaaaay-o. Daylight come and me wan' go home." The group of people in front of us turned around to see who the crazy woman was singing in the back of church. At this point, I felt like I had to back her play. I replied, "Day, me say Day, me say Day, me say Daaaaaay-o." This went on for a few more seconds. We got all the way to "Lift six-foot, seven-foot, eight-foot bunch," before the usher asked us to stop.

Easter 2018, getting kicked out of church like a Stanuszek.

Always nice to be noticed by your spouse. Like when your wife leans over after dinner and says, "You have some cheese hanging from your double chin."

All the feels.

Fellas, it's best to have that whole "is it ok to piss in the shower?" conversation with your wife early in the relationship. Just get that one out of the way, like in week 1. Don't wait 13 years. If, however, you're like me and you avoid that conversation, but your wife (completely out of the blue) asks if you piss in the master bathroom shower, the answer - and trust me on this - is NO!

Marriage.

Wife: "Stu, I can't believe you just said that. You know, sometimes you can be a real asshole!!!"

Me: "Hey, you want to watch a documentary on cults?"

Wife: "Give me five minutes."

So, I'm standing on the balcony of my hotel room when I notice a slightly inebriated coed walking by (about 12 floors below). She sees me, and in a moment of spontaneity, she flashes me her breasts. Now, this is not the first time I've seen breasts, and I'm damn near 40 years old, so I didn't respond with your typical frat boy, "Whoa!!!," "Oh baby!!!," or "Do it again!!!" No, I went with a very nonchalant, "Thank you." Well, that didn't seem to be enough of a response for the young lady. She yells, "That's all I get? A thank you?" I responded, "Ummm... Thank you..... and ...... let me go get my son so he can see this too?

The couple that I met in the resort's hot tub this morning spoke in a thick Lebanese accent. After some chit chat with the couple, the gentleman turned to me and said, "We fucka! We fucka!" My Lebanese is a little rusty, so I didn't know how to respond. I went with, "No. No. No. You two fucka. Me married. Me no fucka." Just like that, he then carried the conversation on to something mundane, like the weather, and acted like nothing had happened. But we both knew.

In honor of International Women's Day, I left work early to spend a little quality time at home with the wife. Five minutes after arriving home, I - having now realized we would be alone for the next two hours - came up with a fun and "delightful" little plan for the afternoon. Three minutes later, my wife - having now figured out my plan - sent me back to work.

Mommy walks to the mailbox for 30 seconds of alone time. Children lose their shit due to separation anxiety.

Daddy leaves home for a 10-day business trip. Children forget what he looks like an hour later; call dibs for his side of the bed.

Lying in bed with my wife, Mandy, and seeing that none of my lines are working tonight, I go for broke:

Me: "So, what would happen if I ripped off my underwear right now. What would that get me?"

Wife: "A cold, maybe."

I reached the conclusion about 10 minutes ago that parents don't buy bigger and bigger houses over the years because they have more and more stuff to store. Parents buy bigger and bigger houses to put more and more distance between them and their kids.

When a man finds a pair of underwear that fits him just right, he sticks with them thru thick and thin and for better or worse. I mean, I have underwear in my regular rotation that have outlasted many of my friends' marriages. So, when the elastic on the band of an old favorite wears out beyond repair, you can't expect him to just throw them out.

Dad: "Stu, what the hell is that blue cloth sticking out from under your shorts?"

Me: "An old friend, pops. An old friend."

That moment at your daughter's Catholic school fundraiser when - after about three hours of drinking - the DJ unexpectedly plays Ginuwine's "My pony," and the 20 or so fourth grade moms in attendance - each of whom had been relatively calm up to that point - had this look come over their faces like, "We're owning this dance floor tonight like it's 1997, bitches."

As for the rest of the night ..... well ...... let's just say the church's confessional was full this morning.

Marky Mark's "Good Vibrations" came on the radio last Friday morning as I was driving my kids to school. My daughter just sat there, completely uninterested in the song. She looked almost annoyed by it. On Tuesday, I showed her a picture of Mark Wahlberg, and told her that he was the guy singing the song. She seemed very surprised (as she stared at his picture for a few minutes). This morning, "Good Vibrations" came on the radio again. This time, my daughter immediately recognized it, and spent 3 1/2 minutes bouncing around in her chair, twirling her hair, and humming away. It was the same look my wife gets when she sees Robert Downey, Jr.

Damn you Mark Wahlberg, with your toned abs and your Boston accent. Damn you!

The priest told us this morning that Fridays during Lent are supposed to be days of abstinence. Priests can't get married, of course, so perhaps they don't realize this, but for most of us married men, practically every day is a day of abstinence. And if I'm being honest, my wife appears to be pretty excited about making sure that we comply with the priest's directive. You know, for Jesus and all.

For our first child, a girl, my wife, Mandy, decorated this 150-page baby book which is bursting at the seams with photos, drawings, baby teeth, and cute devotionals to remember all her little milestones.

For our second child, a boy, my wife paper clipped a lock of his hair to an envelope and called it good.

Backing into a parked car - bad.

Backing into a parked car in front of your wife - much, much badder.

Got a buddy who thinks he just went through the worst break up of his life because his girlfriend admitted to lying all these years about liking his cooking. I'm thinking, "Really?!? That's the worst break up of your life?" I had a woman once brag to me that she had faked narcolepsy for a year to have an excuse to get out of the hibity dibity.

Pretty sure I got him beat.

Blackstreet's "No Diggity" came on during the Friday Morning Throwback this morning. That song came out just as I was sowing my wild oats in college, so whenever it comes on the radio, I think of my ol' frat house and the lovely ladies who would frequent it. Especially, the ladies. So, so many ladies. So, when it came on this morning in my car, I looked back at my son and he's bobbing his head. I'm thinking, "Boy, you're going to have such a great time in college." Then I peer over at my daughter - who is also bobbing her head - and I think, "Oh shit!"

The boy finally learned how to wipe his own ass tonight. Facebook, you have my permission to remind me of this "Memory" in like 7 years, so I can embarrass the hell out of him.

Having a grand old time at family dinner tonight listening to my son talk about his new imaginary friend, "Flack." After about 10 minutes, the boy stands up and exclaims, "And Flack has a big ol' butt..." I, of course, start laughing because .... well ... I'm immature. The boy pauses for about 5 seconds and then he finishes his sentence, "..... like mommy."

The mood at family dinner changed considerably after that point.

For any men out there, who want to use a bathroom stall at the restaurant off Merchants Drive, I must apologize. My boy thought it was funny to lock himself in the first stall. When he realized that Daddy couldn't fit under the stall door, he proceeded to army crawl from stall to stall locking each of the doors from the inside. Four stalls, four locked doors. I know I'm supposed to be mad at the boy, but damn! This kid is entertaining.

My wife and I missed that whole "I'm gonna text you a half-naked picture of myself so you can fantasize about me at work and hopefully you won't show your buddies these pics when you're drunk one day" phase. Instead, we just send each other pictures of food.

Difference between having boys vs. having girls:

Me: "Gracie, Daddy loves you."

Gracie: "I love you too, Daddy."

Me: "Huck, Daddy loves you."

Huck: "Poopy pickle popsicle."

As a father, this guy was a damn dumpster fire. I mean, a three at best. But as a wordsmith - with him repeatedly referring to his Johnson as his "pleasure hammer" - this guy was a ten.

Dog got neutered today. First time I've felt the dog and me had anything in common.

I'd do anything for my wife. I'd walk through fire. I'd take a bullet. I'd lie, cheat, and steal. Anything ..... except hang our Christmas decorations before Thanksgiving. On that, I draw a line.

The kids are going through the Target catalog and circling the toys they want from Santa. I remember doing that as a kid, too. Though in my day, instead of Target, it was JC Penny's, and instead of toys, it was the ladies in the back of the catalog in their bras.

To Cletus, the drive thru worker, who - out of spite - gave my son a Happy Meal with a girl's toy when I clearly asked for a Happy Meal with a boy's toy: my son has a sister, asshole. This Hello Kitty teapot is worth 15 army guys on the brother/sister black market.

Though I hate leaving these little weekend getaways, I love it when the wife reminds me (about two hours before checking out) that if these snacks aren't eaten by the time we leave, they're getting tossed. She just opens the fridge and says, "Handle your business, Sir."

So, I found myself walking down the adult hygiene aisle at the grocery store (where they keep the adult diapers) when a 16-year-old male employee decided to mess with me. I thought this could be fun.

High schooler: "Sir, can I help you pick out an adult undergarment?"

..... Pause ......

Me: "Oh yeah, I piss myself all the time! Looking for something in a low rise, bikini. Preferably with cheetah print. You got anything like that?"

My wife's cat has been missing since we moved two weeks ago. If you see a black and white skunk-lookin' cat with the disposition of a real asshole, feel free to keep him. I just don't know if I could take losing him again.

I may catch hell for this, but for the life of me, I don't get why attractive women post pictures on Facebook using filters which make their skin look unrealistically unblemished, and their faces look impossibly slim. When I see them, all I can think of are the people in Soundgarden's "Black Hole Sun" music video.

The way my son pouts when my wife says he can't have a cookie is apparently identical to the way I pout when my wife says I can't have ...... well, something else.

When it comes to sprinting, Carl Lewis I am not. However, I learned tonight that when iTunes decides to randomly switch the music I was playing for my girls soccer team from the fun, happy "soccer mix" I was playing to the testosterone filled, aggressive "workout mix" I play at the gym, I can sprint from one end of the soccer field to the other like Usain Bolt. On the bright side, not a lot of eight-year old girls in East Tennessee have heard Dayton Family's song "Flint town," so there's that....

I walk in to the room just as my mom is giving my daughter a hint for the next word on her spelling test. My mom says, "Now Gracie, it starts with an 's.' If you need two eggs, but you only have one." I whisper to my daughter my suggestion. "No daddy, that isn't right," she giggles.

Apparently, the teacher opted to go with "shortage" this week. I still think "shit out of luck" works better.

I came home tonight to find two gallons of local milk sitting in my fridge; each priced at $6.99 a gallon. I'm not from around here so I don't have this affinity for this farm like my wife does, but at that price, their cows must shit gold or deal poker or something.

I'm married to an intelligent, sexy, vivacious woman, who apparently has been hiding a secret from me for 16 years:

Wife: "So, why do we get a facedown card anyway?"

Me: "Honey, it's Black Jack. We've played this game thousands of times. In tournaments. At parties. For money. You mean to tell me that after all these years, you never knew to add the facedown card with the faceup card? What did you think the facedown card was there for anyway?"

Wife: [very long pause] "As kinda like a coaster for the faceup card in case someone spills a drink."

Our whole marriage has been a sham.

The little boy hit the little girl, and my little boy, Huck, put the other little boy on his ass because of it. My wife told Huck that he shouldn't hit other little boys
....

I had a different response.

Wanted: gay man to occasionally hang out with my wife so she can have adult man/woman conversations about food, fashion, makeup, hair styles, books, romantic comedies, and current events. Wife is particularly looking for a man who doesn't relate everything back to a football analogy, and who has read more fiction than just Dr. Seuss and Shel Silverstein. Pay is negotiable.

When you ask your wife if you can change your pet name for her from "Babe" to "Puddin'," don't expect her to say yes. Relatedly, if you go ahead and do it anyway, expect your wife - somewhere between the 5th and 6th "Puddin'," to kick you out of the bedroom for the foreseeable future.

So, I pulled up next to your basic 40-year-old white boy, who's stopped at a red light in his Honda Civic, with his windows down, and rap music blasting from his radio (and it wasn't even good rap music). Now, I have no problem with his windows down and his music blasting (I do that all the time), but what got me was that this middle-aged white boy was trying so hard to look ... well .... hard. I figured someone had to do something to let this guy know how ridiculous he looked. So, I rolled my windows down, cranked up the "Footloose" soundtrack loud enough to get his attention, and did my level best to imitate Kevin Bacon's prom dance scene (from the movie) from my driver's seat. The guy noticed and started shaking his head left and right (looking as hard as he could). Light turned green, and he gunned it. I met him at the next red light though; only this time I've changed the song to "Let's hear it for the boy!" Like before, I did my level best to imitate Chris Penn's dance scene from the movie from my driver's seat. Guy cracked a smile this time. But again, he gunned it when the light turned green. I caught up to him one last time; I figured I needed to go big this time or go home. So, I pulled up to the red light with "Almost Paradise" blasting from my radio. He started laughing, and absolutely lost it when I did my signature "jazz hands."

Showed him!

www.ingramcontent.com/pod-product-compliance
Lightning Source LLC
Chambersburg PA
CBHW032045290426
44110CB00012B/966